Validations

Henry Arguelles

Natalie and Logan: you two have always been my light, my warmth, and my home. Thank you both for being you.

Contents

Sharp Words

Please...stop talking.

I know this is the end
and I'm not arguing
or trying to pretend
that there's any hope
- you've made it clear -
that this relationship is broken
and our end is near.

I've accepted that I
am not what you need
but please stop cutting me down;

why do I have to bleed?

Was It Worth It?

It was worth the price I paid
to know the passion in your touch,
but I can't afford to know it again;
the last time cost too much.

Validate Yourself

I have so much love
to give to someone else,
but I haven't found my person
so I've learned to love myself.

Cliché Deconstruction #9

Don't trust anyone
that promises the stars,
because even the Moon
is too goddamn far.

Just Me And My Shovel

Every time I think the hole I'm in
cannot possibly get any deeper,
I look up at the distant sky and say:
"Damnit: that Sun just gets further away."

That Last Communication

I wasn't worth the drive
but you said a call was fine
because driving to me
would take up too much of your time
but then the call was too much
because you'd had a long day
and a text would be enough
to say what you had to say
but then the text never happened -
maybe you were tired...

there was no need to ghost me:
I already knew I wasn't desired.

Audience Required

I thought I was special
because you kept sending me selfies,
but not once did you ever
ask for any of me.

And then you would text me
constantly about your day,
but when I tried talking about mine
you had little to say.

I held on to every detail,
any little thing you wanted to share, but
you never knew my thoughts and dreams-
never asked, never really cared.

I should have realized then
what is now obvious:
you never really wanted a partner-
you just needed an audience.

Fear = Courage

Bravery is a quality
that anyone can get
because fear is just courage
you haven't found yet.

Post-Relationship Truth #5

Stupid movies and love songs always
make me give relationships a chance;
they never work out for me because
I keep romanticizing romance.

Life

If I had lived the life
I thought I'd live,
then I wouldn't have lived
a life worth living.

Regret/Longing

We found peace once,
and then that moment passed;
I should have fought harder
to make that moment last.

Me and God (Again)

You wanted my faith,
you wanted my time –
for me to devote a life to you
that is rightfully mine;

I'm supposed to give you my prayers
and entreat to you my pleas
and when I'm at my lowest
I'm to get down on my knees
and open my heart to you
and beg and say please
and in return you'll help me...

as long as you get my fealty.

But when did you guide me
and give me insight?
When have you ever
had my back in a fight?
I'm not scared of the darkness
and I don't need a light
but goddamn I would have liked a sign
just to know it'll be allright.

I tried to believe in you
but it never made a difference,
so I give you what you gave me:

you can have my indifference.

Shoulder Your Load

We broke up as lovers
and tried to be friends
but since we're platonic
the gaslighting doesn't end
because you keep calling me out
for anything I did wrong
while you absolve yourself insisting
you were the victim all along.

I wanted us to be cool
but your friendship's no great loss;
learn to deal with your own problems
instead of having me carry your cross.

How Many Likes For This Poem?

Social media is depressing and
we just want to be noticed,
that's why we rush to like pics
whenever they're posted
and get mad when others
don't like ours in return
and if they don't like and don't comment –
that's a tacit burn.

The need for attention
may be innate and primal
but it's sad that we define significance
by whether or not we go viral.

Moment

Some moments
can last for
a lifetime
and
some moments
should last us
forever
but
with you each
moment is
a lifetime
and
I need that
moment to
come to an
end.

Gonna Do Things Easier From Now On

I know one reason why I wasn't able
to live the life I wanted to live:
so much energy spent punishing everyone
when it was so much easier to forgive.

Mine, All Mine!

I have my peace -
go find your own;
don't try to take from me
what I fought for alone.

A Narcissist During A Conversation

I didn't hear you talking
because I had something to say
and your thoughts were important, sure
but they just got in the way
of me dropping that insight
I was sure you wanted to hear:
if you didn't want my opinion,
why are you even here?!?

Dichotomies

I am a storm and
I am a clear sky;

I have been the spider
and I have been the fly.

I've had my heartbroken
and I've broken hearts;

I have helped people grow
and I've torn them apart.

I fully embrace
the contradictions in me
because life is defined
by its dichotomies.

Jigsaw Puzzles

The beauty of
a jigsaw puzzle
is that you don't
need every piece
to see the whole
picture completely.

Glass

My skin is glass:
you can see right through me
but if you want to touch me,
be careful:

I break easily.

Cliché Deconstruction #104

They say we fear
what we do not know
which is why so many of us
never get to know ourselves.

Must Get Taller

Every time I think
I've outgrown my insecurities,
I look up and there they are,
overshadowing me.

Nietzsche + Empathy

When I gazed into the abyss,
the abyss gazed back,
and right then I knew
that there was nothing to fear from
the dark because it
was just lonely too.

Transparency

It's not me
that you're dying to see;
you're just trying to sate
your need to be seen.

You Can Stop Castigating Me Now; I Get It

...yeah, this
was my choice and
yeah, I
have to own it,
but damn:
didn't think so much
could change
in a single
moment!

You Were the Strong One

I had no faith in the future –
I needed proof;
I thought you were naive
for not seeing the truth
that our life together
wouldn't work out
and that the current problems we had
would continue throughout.

I had become very negative
over the past few years
and I let my insecurities
empower my fears
so when we broke up
I acted all tough,
claiming that even though I loved you
love just wouldn't be enough.

But now I understand
just how and why I was wrong:

I was a coward that ran
while you were always strong
for believing in us
and trying to hold on;
I had to end up alone
to realize where I belong.

Paradox

Breakups either
make no sense

OR

they make all the sense
in the world and you were a fool
for not doing it sooner and how could you
have missed the signs and now you're
much better off without them and
this is your time to rediscover
yourself and grow.

Don't Hoard Emotions

Get rid of those
feelings you don't need,
won't use again,
have gone out of style,
serve no purpose,
and can be replaced
with fresher and
better emotions.

If all you do
is hold on to how
you felt, then how
can you ever feel
anything new?

Because I'm Stubborn

I carry the world
on my shoulders;
wouldn't be too heavy
but for the chip
I refuse to drop.

Either Way I Lose

Too much pressure for me to handle -
I'm about to explode;
no one can ever see me like this -
I would rather implode.

I'm Not Chill About Love

I can't just let this
be what it will be;
a tumultuous life has left me
with too much insecurity.

I wish I could just live in the moment
but I don't have the ability
to invest my heart
where there's so much uncertainty.

Back

You don't have
to have my back;
I just need you
to get off my back
because I'm leaving all this
and not coming back
and neither you nor anyone
will ever hold me back

again.

Cliché Deconstruction #64

If life's a beach,
then dreams are sand
- millions of grains all around -
but as the waves
wash sand away,
all that's left is solid ground.

Self-Reflection #26

I never learned how to get help
and I didn't think I could be wrong,
which is why I was vengeful:
it's easier to be hurt and
to make others feel your pain too
than to admit you're just resentful.

Thoughts Before Bed (Sometimes)

Before I fall asleep I hope
that it will be my last night,
because every day has been a struggle
and I think I've earned the right
to quit this painful life
that I've held on to for far too long,
because no matter how hard I've tried
I can't find where I belong.

That Social Media Life

It seems like we all
just want to be seen,
to have people hawk us
from their tiny screens
and to obsess over
our each and every move
ready with a comment praising us
and just as ready to reprove.

I'm sure its intoxicating
to be well known
but it's sad that our main goal in life
is to be on everyone's phone.

I Don't Think There Will Be A Next Time Though

Why are you mad:
because I broke your heart
or because I
broke your expectations?

Maybe next time,
see me as a person
and not as a
project or assignment.

Guess It WAS Me After All

I thought you became boring
but once again I was wrong:
you had no energy left
after trying to be all
of the things I expected
and required you to be;
I never saw you because
it's always all about me.

Weekly Routine

I cry at least
once a week;
no one sees it...

no one sees I'm weak.

True Happiness

This pursuit of happiness
has brought me nothing but
some sadness and resentment;
I was wrong to search for more
and should have decided
to be happy with contentment.

So Much For Prayer...

I opened my heart
to God before,
but God said "NO!"
and just shut that door.

Brrr

Some nights are
a two-blanket kind of night;
the weather's
irrelevant when the cold
comes from you.

And Thank You

I
don't have
anything
left to give but
what I have left is
yours to take but
I don't want
you to
take
it and
leave me with
nothing again
and I don't know why
you keep coming
back to me
or why
I
let you
but I can't
keep doing this
because I'm not strong
enough to tell
you to go
away

and
never
come back so
I'll beg and plead
that you finally
show me mercy
and stay out
of my
life
but you
won't listen
and I'm tired
of asking for you
to respect me
or show me
kindness
so
I will
take what's mine:
my sense of self
and my sense of pride,
and tell (not ask)
you to stay
away
from

me and
leave me be
because I don't
want you anymore
and you do not
deserve me
so I'll
ask
you to
kindly get
the hell out of
my life but because
I have class, I'll
be polite
and say
"please."

Hopeful Romantic

I don't like
the term
"hopeless romantic"
because it
implies
that I've lost all hope;

I prefer
the term
"hopeful romantic"
because it
implies
I've still got a shot.

Samsara Sucks – a Microplay

This microplay takes place in the Afterlife, and I am about to reincarnate.

Act One, Scene One

God: You did good that last time, you learned what life's about...

Me: *(interrupting)* Yeah, but it wasn't worth it; think I'll sit this one out.

Perception

We had a brief chance at happiness
and then we had none;
guess we didn't have a relationship -
just the promise of one.

Getting Older

Life pushed me forward
and I had to leave my dreams behind,
and now that I can get them back
I don't think I'll have the time.

Mindreader/Partner

So...

I'm supposed
to know your every thought
and to not push your buttons
so that fights don't get fought
and I'm to be tender
yet assertive and rough
and to know how far to go
without you saying "that's enough;"
I'm to read your mind
and to know your soul,
to instinctively know
how to play my role,
and to know what to do
and exactly what to say
and to automatically anticipate
your needs day-to-day?

Ok.

Cliché Deconstruction #8

People that claim
"God has a plan"
are people whose lives are
going according to plan.

Degrees

I don't feel like I'll ever
truly be who I wanted to be,
and if you don't live your life fully,
you slowly die by degrees.

Too Real?

Meet you at the bar
sometime around 8;
it's time for another
generic first date;
talk for a bit,
we really don't click-
really wish I could
just leave here quick,
but I don't want
to leave and be rude,
so I'll stay even though
I'm not in the mood

but...

what if you
also want this date to conclude?
What if we share
the same attitude
that neither us are evil
but between us there's no magic
and walking away amicably
doesn't have to be tragic?

How nice would it be
to just say to each other straight:
we seem nice and all
but we're not each other's Fate.

Small Mercies

These feelings hurt...
they just won't fade;
I'd hurt more though
if you had stayed.

Fame Is Overrated

I'll never understand
why people idolize celebrities;
sure, they may be rich but
they can't really afford to be free.

I Just Want to Buy a House

I worked long and hard,
studied a worthwhile trade,
and have tried my best
to get by, do right, and save,
but there's no point to all that
because every move I made
put me further in debt
and unable to pay
into this ideal
that we're all supposed to share
but for decades has not been
balanced and fair
except to a select few
or those lucky to be born heirs;
for a lot of us, though,
the American dream is a nightmare.

It's Not The Lottery But...

An unexpected bonus
to being depressed:
I no longer have
a fear of death.

Not a Rhetorical Question

Do I date because
I want someone to love me?
Or am I just tired
of always feeling lonely?

Shards

The stronger I get
the more brittle I become
but when I do snap
under the weight and the stress
there'll be countless shards
everywhere, cutting those that
try to pick them up.

I always draw blood from those
that would bleed for me.

I can only hurt you if
you get close to me
so please, keep your distance and
don't try to touch me.

More Than Atlas

Bearing the weight of the world
is how the Universe burdened me
in a misguided attempt
to make me bend the knee,
but I'm too stupid to quit
and I won't go down easily;
my strength is beyond myth:
Atlas is nothing compared to me!

A Regret Explained

I quit on us
but I never quit
on the idea of us,
and that is why
I constantly think
about us together.

Solo Soy Humano

Me cansé
de mi llanto
porque contigo yo
sufrí tanto;
jamás quería
ser tu santo.

Do We Really Wanna Do This Again Or Are We Just Lonely?

We tried this once
and it didn't work then;
why would it work now?
Just because some time
passed before we tried again
doesn't mean we've figured out how.

Introspection Is Scary

We fear what
we do not know,
why is why
we never try
to know who
we really are.

Post-Relationship Truth #6

Why so quick
to post a pic
and even faster taking it down?
Because all they wanted
was to show others
that they had someone around.

Cliché Deconstruction #26

I will never again carry a torch
because I finally learned
that holding a flame that close to you
only leaves you burned.

Agree To Disagree

Tact.
Civility.
Decorum.
Boundaries.

These constructs exist
to maintain social harmony.

But we're not the UN
and I'm not here for diplomacy:
we can and should be respectful,
but if we have to talk angrily
and get loud and get worked up
and argue to the point of hostility,
I'm cool with that because
seeing eye to eye is key.
In this relationship I want nothing more
than to never feel anxiety
that my partner doesn't have my back
or that they have it by degrees,
so let's talk things out
with passion and with empathy
but's let's come to a consensus
and never agree to disagree.

I Don't Think I'm Negative

It's not that my soul is dark;
it's just that my inner light
casts a hell of a shadow.

God Didn't Answer, But Maybe You Can

If your god
cannot be asked questions,
than how can
your god give you answers?

Yeah...No

I have
so much
to share
with you
but what if
something
happens
and you
don't like
what I share?

Or worse:
you don't
like me
or you
stop liking
me and
I have
to start
over
dating again?

No thanks:
I'm not
sharing
again
and I'm not
about
to let
myself
feel that
rejection.

Want More Vs. Need More

You know what's the problem
with trying to sate a need?
Knowing how much is necessary
and how much of it is greed.

Me Thinking About Aging

My hair is now gray...
wrinkles showing on my face...
time to let the dream die and accept
that I'll never be in a high-speed chase.

It's Not Just Companionship

Every relationship
would be better if
we were up front about the
insecurities
we all have and just stated
from the beginning
what we need to feel fulfilled
instead of acting
as if we are all complete
because if we were
then why would we have to date?

We all want someone
to give us validation
and help us feel like
we're not completely messed up.

Avoid Rebounders

You asked me to hold on
and wait for you to know
what you wanted out of us
and whether we could grow
as a couple and a team
combining our respective lives
but all you really wanted
was for me to help you survive
as you rebounded from your ex
and needed someone safe;
you knew we had no future
while I kept the faith
that we had a chance
at making things work
but when you were sated you left
and now I feel like a jerk.

It really isn't fair
to tell someone you want to go slow
when you know that once you're done
you plan on letting go.

Partnership Is Hard

Sometimes we are
nothing more than assets,
sometimes we are
just some accessories...
but why can't we
be each other's allies?

This Fire's Not For You

I'm still carrying a torch
but this fire isn't for you;
I just don't want to go back
to the cold and the darkness.

Grudge

I'm mad about something
and I can't let it go;
my name has been sullied
and I need the offender to know
that the injury they inflicted
is something I will always feel...

but if I'm being honest...

it shouldn't be that big a deal.

I tend to be dramatic
when my feelings get hurt
and instead of just letting go
I'll work hard to exert
as much energy as possible
to make sure the other person's aware
of how mad I am
(because I really care)
but I'm too prideful to forgive
and too emotional to forget
so instead of moving forward in peace
I move backwards and regress

into a childish way
of dealing with the problem
and instead of rising up,
my resolution skills hit rock bottom.
But I don't know how to move forward
and I don't know how to move on
so either I forget the grudge
or one of us ends up gone
from the other's life
over something trivial;

I should learn to be less rigid;
few things are unforgivable.

I know grudges are stupid
and this isn't who I want to be
but the harder I try to let it go
the harder the grudge holds on to me.

Grass Is Greener And All That

I broke up with you
because you lived too far away;
I wanted someone in my life
I'd be able to see every day.
And now that I'm alone
and you're no longer mine
I see that life was better with you
even if it was only better half the time.

Being Vulnerable

I need to know
if I let go
will you be there
to catch me?
Because I need a break
and I don't know
how much more I can take…
I'm asking you to help me.

Trash

I'm broken and shattered;
pieces of me lie all around,
but don't bother picking them up:
they belong on the ground.

Cliché Deconstruction #139

You said I was
"hot like fire"
and you were right:
all you wanted
from me was warmth
and instead I
burned you, charred you,
consumed your love,
and used it to
feed my own flame.

Now my flame is
just a flicker;
better to let
me put myself
out and then stomp
on the embers
until just smoke
and ash remain
and there's nothing
to reignite.

I thought I was
an inferno,
but the truth is
I am just a
meager cinder.

I'm Romantic Like That

Dating is never easy
but I like to be grownup;
that's why I skip the whole relationship thing
and get straight to the breakup.

I'll usually end a relationship
before it ever really starts;
it's better to minimize the damage
to my impending broken heart.

And all the time I'll spend
regretting and trying to reconnect
can be better spent independently
moving on and learning to forget.

Life has shown me that I can't
make real a fantasy,
because no matter how hard I've tried,
romance doesn't beat reality.

Post-Breakup Realization

You think that it's you
that I'm angry with?

No, I'm angry at myself
for not having the strength
to give us a chance
and let the future play out;
our love was strong
but not as strong as my doubt.

That's Why It's Never Quiet

In the silence
we find ourselves,
and that is why

usually

we tend to have
some kind of noise
in the background.

I Gaslit You Then But I Know Better Now

Then:

These thoughts are gossamer -
pay them no mind;
consider the breadth of my actions
and weigh them in kind.

Now:

These thoughts that we hide
and restrain within
can eventually manifest;
their threat is genuine.

Still Angry

I watched you throw away happiness
with both hands
and then I watched you ruin your life;

things didn't go as planned?

I take no joy in your misery
and I hope you understand
I'm just happy that at the end
I won't be the one holding your hand.

Try Some Empathy

The worst thing you ever said
was that I was always negative;
for a long time I was struggling
and wished you'd be as sensitive
and understanding and helpful
as you claimed yourself to be –
I could have been more optimistic, true,
and you could have tried some empathy.

Ugh: Positive Feelings

Whenever you feel
that how you feel
is something to repress,
then that's exactly the moment
when you need to be extra
and make sure that you express
all the beauty and
all the magic
that show the world who you are,
because there's no need
to be a celebrity
to be a superstar!

Reflection On Dating #17

Why do we go back
to those we dated before?
Because meeting someone new
is such a goddamn chore.

A Very Specific Insight

People that buy books
they have no intention to read
are the kind of people that fault others
for not being what they need.

Intentions And All That

I don't think
you wanted to hurt me,
but when you left me
I was a mess;
even though
it wasn't intentional,
that doesn't mean
it hurt me any less.

Cliché Deconstruction #37

They say if you love someone, let them go,
and if they come back it's meant to be,
but if they don't come back, whose fault is it?

It's yours, for acting stupidly.

Maintaining a relationship is hard enough
without putting it through a stupid test;
fight for someone while they're here,
not after they've already left.

Breakup, Defined:

Someone or
something is
going to break
and there's no
way you can
keep that from
happening.

Update Your Playlist

When you spend all your time
listening to love songs
because you're on your own,
you'll eventually
become convinced that you
will always be alone.

Stalling

I stand strong

against the wind,
against the rain,
against the lightning,
against the pain.

None of that
has killed me yet,
but it's only a matter of time:
storms have no regrets.

Pfft, Psychopomp

You can't scare me, Death –
of you I have no fear.
All that's left to take is my life;
I've already lost what I held dear.

So come and get me whenever you want-
I won't try to hide;
do your job and bring the end
to one that's died inside.

Mistaken Identity

Someone asked me
if I knew you
and I started
to say "yes" but
then I started
thinking about
all the lies and
all the cheating
and the fighting
and the beating
and it turns out
that I never
knew you at all.

Self-Reflection #37

I wish I had
half the chill
I
think I do

instead of all
the anger
I
think I don't.

Lonely

I don't fit in;
I don't belong;
I try to live right
but my life feels wrong.

I don't want to be famous;
I don't want to be known;
I just want to stop feeling like
I'm all

alone.

Yay Me

Another failed relationship but
at least they were to blame…
is that true though?

It seems like it's always the same:

I'm in a relationship
and I always think I'm right;
now I'm alone (again) but hey:

at least I won the fight.

Sycophant

I've held your purse;
I've held your hand;
I've hurt my hands applauding you
because I'm your biggest fan,
but you never reciprocated
and I finally understand
that you didn't want a partner:
you just needed a sycophant.

Let's Not Be Friends

I know you want to
but we can't be friends;
after all, there was a reason
why our relationship came to an end.

I too thought that we were meant
-in some capacity-
to be in each other's lives
but in actuality
I see that all you want
is to castigate me
and that the friendship you offered
is just to appease your egocentricity.

You don't really care about
who I was or who I am:
every time I try sharing my feelings
you don't give a damn;
you constantly rail at me,
listing every real and supposed offence
and I'm just supposed to take it?

That makes no sense.

You've listed all my flaws
and how I'm the one that needs to change
but after listening and thinking about it
I can't help but find it strange
that anything I try to tell you
is automatically rejected or deflected;
instead of our conversations being cathartic
they leave me feeling dejected.

Meanwhile, you demand that I
validate every single thing you say
as if I was some thoughtless automaton
that is obligated to obey.

You know, I actually listened to you
and am trying positivity whenever I can
but no matter how hard I try
I just can't understand
why the entirety of our relationship
is filtered through your perspective
and why I'm the only one here
that's trying to be introspective.

We're neither lovers nor friends
so let's try something new:
never contact me again and
you just keep on doing you.

The Visionary

I dumped you after just a few months
because I saw no future together
and I thought that soon enough I'd find
someone that was smarter, hotter – better.

And here I am, a few years later
- dumber, uglier, and very alone -
but you have definitely moved on
and that's good – you deserve someone that's
grown.

You needed to be perfect to me
because the future was always scary,
and I let myself be led by doubts
while you were always the visionary.

Do. The. Work.

It's not up to someone else
to heal your heart
and put back together
what someone else tore apart.
A new love can help
but the healing starts with you
and you can't hide from it forever
by being with someone new.

Middle-Aged Dating

Before the kids and careers,
the divorces and the pain,
we were hopeful, idealistic
and receptive to change,
but as we got older
our lives became locked
and now we're unwilling to have
our structure get rocked
and so we date constantly
refusing to quit
and trying futilely to find
someone that fits
into the established order
of our now-static lives
and when it doesn't work out
we turn to lies
and tell ourselves
that it just wasn't right
but with every failed relationship
we put up less of a fight
to make it work
and to figure it out;

in our older age
we think we can do without
the work that it takes
to make something last;
we want the eternal
but we want it fast
and we don't recognize our impatience
and how we're always in a hurry-
that's why we drop someone quickly
if we deem them unworthy
and that's where we mess up
and where we need to do better:
we need to let love flow to see
if it's only for a minute or forever.

It's a problem we have,
being driven by this hunger:
we crave our happily ever after
because we're not getting any younger.

We Don't Need To Hang Out

I refuse to sit
and reminisce
about the times
we used to share
because all that mess
I was over with
when you looked
for love elsewhere.

Self-Reflection #53

I kept you at a distance and
I pushed you away;
you fought so hard for us
but I was too weak to stay.

We never got to know
just how special we could be
because now you've moved on
and that's entirely on me.

Hooray For Loneliness!

I'm glad no one is here
to see the real me
because I don't want their concern
and I don't need their pity.

I never wanted to be alone
but now it's obvious
that it's easier getting through life
without an audience.

A Message To My Personal Demons

The rage and the sadness,
the grudges and insecurities -
I keep them hidden inside
so that others never see
the personal demons
that refuse to let me be
and attack my defenses,
wanting to be set free.

I didn't overcome so much in life
just to end up on my knees,
so go to Hell, demons:
you'll never take control of me.

This Narcissist Sincerely Thanks You

After my half-assed romantic gesture
failed spectacularly,
I was way more surprised than hurt you didn't
fall crying at my feet.

I think I cared for you but I know that
I'm more in love with me;
your rejection helped me to uncover
my latent vanity.

Poeticism, Deconstructed

This isn't a poem:
it's just a sentence
that's been formatted
a certain way to
seem deep and full of
meaning but ends up
coming across as
a bit pretentious.